Philip Larkin

An Outsider Poet

Transcending solitude, sex and the ordinary

Fadhil Assultani

Mira Publishing House CIC.
PO BOX 312
Leeds LS16 0FN
West Yorkshire
England
www.MiraPublishing.com

Philip Larkin an Outsider Poet
Transcending solitude, sex and the ordinary
By Fadhil Assultani
ISBN: 978-1-908509-05-5
First published in Great Britain 2013 by Mira Publishing
House CIC.

Printed and bound by Book Empire – Harrogate - UK
Copyright © 2013 Fadhil Assultani

A full CIP record for this book is available from the British
Library.
A full CIP record for this book is available from the Library
of Congress.

Acknowledgements

I would like to express my utmost gratitude and heartfelt thanks to my supervisor Kate McLoughlin from Birkbeck College for her stimulating suggestions and much-needed advice. I am deeply indebted to her. I also want to thank my editor Aiden O'Reilly at Mira publishing house, who raised a number of helpful queries, as well as pointed out some necessary changes. Especially, I would like to give my special thanks to my friend Sian Williams, who kindly read the whole manuscript, and whose insightful incisive comments on the early draft of the book were very helpful. Special thanks also go to my friends Luay Abdulilah and Sophia Tillie for their essential enthusiasm, and interest throughout the whole period of my study.

Philip Larkin
An Outsider Poet

Contents

PREFACE

Larkin and Assultani: Several points in common

By: Amir Taheri

As a reader of poetry for decades, I have always wondered how one poet might read another poet, especially across frontiers set by languages. It was, therefore, no surprise that Fadhil Assultani's dissertation on Philip Larkin came to me as a treat. In fact, it was a special treat for two reasons. First because I have been a fan of Larkin since, as a student in London, I discovered him in the 1960s. Next, in the 1990s, I had the pleasure of making Fadhil Assultani's friendship which, in turn, gave me the privilege of being among the first readers of his poems as he committed them to paper.

Although they hail from different horizons, Larkin and Assultani have several points in common. Both are products of cultures in which poetry is still of great importance. In my first encounter with Britain I was surprised by the fact that, compared to other European countries that I knew including France and Germany, poetry attracted large audiences. I remember attending one "reading" by Adrian Mitchell that had attracted over

1

3000 people in one of London's central parks. Several poets were household names and, in some cases, treated almost like rock stars with all the advantages and disadvantages of such treatment, including unwelcome attention from the tabloids. What T.S Eliot had famously called a "minor art form" appeared to have a major impact on the nation's cultural undercurrents. In an obviously different context, poetry enjoys the same prestige in Iraq, Assultani's native land. In a sense, one might even claim that it was in Iraq, the ancient Mesopotamia, where the epic of Gilgamesh marked the birth of literature as deeply felt human response to the mysteries of existence. Again in the 1960s, outside the narrow circle of the ruling elite the only Iraqis known to the proverbial man in the street were poets, many of them already in exile.

From the start, I saw Larkin's work as a poetical version of chamber music. He is the poet of small touches, fleeting moments, and flashes of insight, the poet of enduring transience as formulated in "Modesties", one of his shortest poems. For his part, Assultani, especially in his poems written in the past decade or so, has distanced himself from the epic ambitions of many Arab poets of his generation and moved closer to what Rene Char called "the small music of life."

2

Even at first glance, Larkin appears as an outsider. The poets of the generation immediately before him had encountered strong ideological currents, from Auden's hybrid leftism to Eliot's Anglo-Catholicism.

Some had pushed their ways into the major events of their time, including the two world wars and the Spanish Civil War. Many more had sought experience and adventure in distant lands, in some cases continuing the Byronic tradition. Larkin, however, was as stationary as an oak tree on the tip of the forest. For decades he lived in Hull, not the most cosmopolitan city in Great Britain, taking only a few days to visit friends in even quieter places in South Wales. In a sense, Larkin resided in his solitude, a universe that, although some mistook it for loneliness, was vast enough for the development and expression of an amazing array of sentiments. In his dissertation, Assultani examines Larkin's process of "transcending solitude" through poetry.

It was not only away from the fashionable ideologies of the day that Larkin built his outsiderness. He also developed a defence mechanism against the emerging consumer society that, starting from the early 1960s, the era of "You've never had it so good!' was recasting every aspect of Western man's existence.

A practitioner of the "lower-thy-expectation" long before environmentalists made it into a talisman, Larkin remained outside the Sweet Sixties and the sexual revolution it generated.

That Larkin's outsiderness should appear weird to some of his contemporaries is no surprise. In an age of "movements" he insisted on remaining stationary. At a time when ideologies dominated, he was free of all doctrinal straitjackets. The nascent fashion of multiculturalism never touched him as he remained resolutely English. In fact, it was his very Englishness that ensured his universal appeal, making him attractive to, and accessible to, many, including Assultani, from vastly different cultural backgrounds. That some narrow-minded ideologues should see him as "racist" and "misogynist" is no surprise. He was not one for political correctness in any terms. More unjust, however, are the claims that Larkin is the poet of the "vulgar" and the "ordinary". In any case, much of life is "vulgar" and "ordinary". Assultani deals with all such labels in a calm and effective manner. He also takes on the argument that Larkin is either a Nihilist, a charge also levelled against Dostoyevsky, among others, or a conjurer of ambiguity, a label also used against Mallarmé.

Larkin is often mentioned in conjunction with his friend John Betjeman, with the implication that the two were a pair. Some critics also see him as a literary heir to Thomas Hardy, whose poetry initially inspired Larkin. However, in one of the more exciting segments of his study, Assultani identifies affinities between Larkin and another of his favourite British poets, R S Thomas. Assultani writes:

I would argue that Larkin is closer to R.S. Thomas. It might even be claimed that many of Larkin's themes are more analogous with those of Thomas than with any other British poet in the second half of the twentieth century, though their approaches and styles are essentially different. *Waiting, absences, death, failure, suffering, echo, shadows,* and *death* are very common vocabularies in their poetic discourse. It seems that both poets echo ideas of Kierkegaard, perhaps unconsciously in the case of Larkin, and consciously with Thomas who read Kierkegaard and dedicated a poem to him. Both poets are preoccupied with almost the same existentialist themes: outsiderness, freedom of choice, dichotomy between life and art, self and others. But unlike Larkin, the secular, Thomas's approaches to his themes are arguably theological, but his main concern, like Larkin, is the human condition: solitude, absence, frustration, misery and spiritual failure in the materialistic modern society. In their lives and works, both poets seek to solve dichotomy between art and life, between 'two hungers, hunger for bread, and hunger of the uncouth soul for the light's grace', as beautifully expressed by Thomas's poem 'Dark Well'.[44] For both Larkin and Thomas, the question of belonging is the core of their existential philosophy, in the broad sense of the word, whether it takes an arguably empirical perspective, as in the case of Larkin, or a theological form as with Thomas.

Larkin's poetry reached its peak in an historical season dominated by post-Imperial angst, expressed as "looking back in anger." Larkin, however, his poetic gaze directed at "arrogant eternity" never looked back. Assultani's study may well represent the homage that one poet pays to another across generations and cultural boundaries. But it is also a scholarly probe shedding new light on aspects of Larkin's poetry beyond the pseudo-biographised sorties to which he has been subjected for decades. While Assultani's choice of Larkin, as a dissertation subject, is initially rooted in personal taste, it also reflects the abiding stature that the librarian of Hull University has acquired a quarter of a century after his death. Larkin's poetry has stood the test of time, securing for him a place in the pantheon of modern English classics. "I'd like to think ... that people in pubs would talk about my poems", Larkin once wrote. Well, they do, in pubs and in other places.

Introduction

The cultural climate in mid-twentieth century England was not receptive to the techniques of surrealism, nor to the concept of an outsider. In the former case, David Gascoigne was somewhat an exception, and he lived for some time in France where he presumably was influenced by French writers. In the latter, Colin Wilson published his study *The Outsider* in 1956, but it tellingly focuses on foreign writers, apart from T.E. Lawrence and H.G. Wells. For this reason, perhaps, Larkin was not viewed as an outsider, apart from some references to his personal life as a solitary and a bachelor which has nothing to do with the concept of being an outsider in its philosophical interpretation. Larkin wasn't just a loner or a reclusive person. From the beginning, he held his own existentialist views on life, art, society, sex, solitude, selfhood and otherness, belonging, uncertainty, self-realization, anxiety, and undecidedness. Viewed from this perspective, we can't find contradictions in his various stances, but, on the contrary, his work forms one protracted poem, in which he meditates on these big issues occupying humanity in the twentieth century.

For me, Larkin, both as a person and as a poet, is an outsider, in the existentialistic sense of the word, and he is in harmony with himself. There aren't two distinct Larkins, or two sides of him, as many of his critics suggest. By making a comparison of his poetry, prose and his personal letters, we can discern coherent views and visions that govern his seemingly contradictory attitudes. His whole persona, similar to existentialist outsider characters in modern literature, confronts the issues preoccupying his age, such as consciousness, freedom of choice, human knowledge, and selfhood and otherness in modern societies. Confronting these issues, Larkin's approach is neither nihilistic nor pessimistic. He does not negate life, like nihilists, but questions the very nature of our existence in relation to human misery and alienation, and explores the hidden ugliness of our societies and the absurdity of our existence in order to open our eyes and minds to change ourselves and reality for the better. From this point of view, any pessimistic poem is the most optimistic poem in the world, as Larkin once said.

Larkin believed that deprivation is for him what daffodils were for Wordsworth. This is quite true. Deprivation is the dominant theme of his major collections *The Less Deceived* (1955), *The Whitsun*

Wedding (1964), and *High Windows* (1974). It is also the main theme in his collection *Grip of Light*, written in 1947, but never published. But Larkin's deprivation is self-imposed as a path to transcendence, an escape from the consumer world, and an attempt to disengage art from society, and the self from others. It is neither a consequence of psychological disorder, nor of misogyny, narcissist pathology or the discomfort he feels with the shape of the personality he was given, as some critics argue, but rather a product of meditation on selfhood and the decline of post-war society and culture. Throughout this book, we will be examining such meditations and showing how they are reflected in Larkin's poetry and have a close relationship with the development of his poetic experience. By analyzing his early poems dating back even to the 30s, and comparing them with his later poems, we will see that there are coherent existential issues penetrating the poetry from the very beginning.

Larkin's controversial attitudes to women and sex should be understood within the context of those existentialist views expressed in his poetry, and not deduced from Larkin's private life. By analyzing some of his poems, particularly 'High Windows', which is key to understanding Larkin in this regard, and reading the personal letters relevant to the matter, his problems with women and sex can be seen as part of his larger struggle with life as an outsider. The outsider is always indecisive man, unable to act, only react.

In his struggle with life, Larkin sought, like any outsider, to build by a process of transcendence an imaginative alternative to a world he feels he does not belong to. This process of recreating helps Larkin to transcend the objects he faces, the ideas he meditates on, the environment surrounding him, the poet himself, as well as the readers, to the level of the abstract, in which a sense of happiness and liberation from bleak reality and contradictions is felt. Thus he builds an imaginative world, in which the subject and the object are fused into a unity. Larkin uses the physical materials of reality, which he deliberately accumulates, as a bridge to that imaginative world, in which he feels a sense of belonging, and where can say 'this is my proper place'. For this reason, as I have argued in the final chapter, Larkin's poetry is more complicated than some critics suggest, because, firstly, it operates on various existential levels, and secondly, because of the sophisticated process of recreation and transcendence which Larkin employs in his attempts to find answers to the basic questions preoccupying his age and still preoccupying our age. This will be widely discussed in the third chapter, where I deal with the nature of Larkin's poetry in its relationship to the ordinary, comparing his poetry to that of the New York School poets, for example.

Finally, this book is not concerned about whether Larkin is a Movement poet or not, or a modernist poet or not. Larkin once said, 'I do not want to change, just to become better', quoting Oscar Wilde that 'only mediocrities develop'.[1] Indeed, he did not change. He went on writing about the same themes, or precisely one theme concerning his relationship with others, self, society and existence. From an aesthetic point of view, he did indeed progress when he found his own voice, and began writing differently about 1948 or 1949 when he stopped writing 'worthless Yeats-y poems', as he said in an interview with the late poet Ian Hamilton.[2]

Chapter 1

Transcending solitude

In a cartoon that Larkin drew during his late adolescent years, we see that his father, mother and sister are facing each other. {...} The father is reading a newspaper, the mother is knitting, and the sister is standing facing them. What is most striking about the cartoon is that the figure of the young artist is sitting completely outside the family circle, scribbling at a desk with one hand while looking up; his face is turned toward the viewer, suffused with dark emotion, and a huge wordless exclamation point hovers over his head. [1]

There is no difference between this child's world and the adult's. His adulthood is an extension of his experience of childhood, which he describes as 'forgotten boredom' in his poem 'Coming'.[2]

A sense of alienation from the outside world will characterise much of his poetry. In a poem as early as 1938, Larkin wrote: 'A web of drifting mist o'er wood and wold/ As quiet as death' and 'Dark night creeps in, and leaves the world alone' (*CP* 225), or: 'Outside, the

14

forest will bite, thaw, then return/ inside, the candle will burn' (*CP* 233).

1n 1946, he repeated the same theme: '…When I lift/my head, I see the walls have killed the sun/ And light is cold' (*CP* 12). Almost thirty years later, he once again expressed almost exactly the same sense of aloneness and existentialist anxieties in very similar images: 'In shoeless corridors, the lights burnt. How/ Isolated, like a fort, it is-/ The headed paper, made for writing home (If home existed)/ letters of exile. Now/ Nights comes on. Waves fold behind villages' (CP 163).

He confirmed this feeling when he wrote: 'D.H. Lawrence is as important to me as Shakespeare was to Keats because the real message of Lawrence is that: people occasionally; really everyone is alone.' [3] In this period, there was harmony between Larkin and his persona, whether in poetry or prose.

In his two novels, *Jill* [4] and *A Girl in Winter*,[5] the protagonists are outsiders haunted by alienation. In *Jill*, John Kemp comes to Oxford to study, but very soon he develops a sense of alienation. His only refuge is his room. Gradually, Oxford becomes 'an unreal city, until it resembles T.S. Eliot's city in 'The Waste Land''.[6] In *A Girl in Winter*, Katherine is a refugee driven from her country by the war. Both are reluctant to commit

15

themselves to any place, except, perhaps, to their own room, because they cannot find their proper place, as Larkin expresses it in his poem 'Places, Loved Ones': 'No, I have never found/ The place where I could say/ This is my proper ground / Here I shall stay' (*CP* 99). He confirmed this when asked about Hull, where he lived for thirty years, in an interview with *The Observer* in 1979: 'I do not really notice where I live'.[7] Larkin doesn't mean by *place* a geographical location, or a natural environment, but a psychological, cultural and existentialist state. Real place, as the French philosopher Gaston Bachelard beautifully puts it, is 'our corner in the world, {......} our first universe, and a real cosmos in every sense of the world'.[8] For Bachelard, whose influential book, *Aesthetics of Space*, was translated into English in 1964, we inhabit our vital space in accord with all the dialectics of life, and we take roots, day after day. We experience place in its reality and virtuality, through thought and dreams. Hence, it is connected with memory and consciousness, and inhabits imagined as well as actual existence. Bachelard goes on to say:

Place forms our way of living and our understanding of ourselves and others. To describe a place as "home" is also to acknowledge its relationship to ourselves, and to

16

create a mutual sense of belonging. At the same time, the oppressive physical living space can make us feel oppressed. Thus we are positively and negatively influenced by our environment and we take on characteristics of the place (home). [9]

Larkin is like his hero, John Kemp, in *Jill*, who is 'pale with fear as he travels down in the train from his Midlands home to begin his first term - he even eats his sandwiches in the lavatory rather than suffer the scrutiny of his fellow-passengers, not because he is shy like Larkin, as Motion suggests,[10] but because he does not like to be scrutinized. The outsider is a good observer, like Larkin himself, but he cannot bear to be observed by the crowd. He always escapes from the crowd, not because he is anti-life, but because he feels that they threaten his authentic individuality. Kierkegaard views the crowd 'as enemy of true being'.[11] For him, a crowd in its very concept 'is the untruth, by reason of the fact that it renders the individual completely impenitent and irresponsible'.[12]

But Larkin does not dislike the crowd in general. For him, there are two kinds of crowd. The first one is composed of consumers and exploiters, or else of those who are 'all of the mind'. [13] The second one is the ordinary, innocent and spontaneous crowd: with it

17

Larkin not only forgets himself as an outsider, but also celebrates human beauty, as we will see, for example, in 'To the Sea' (*CP* 173) and 'The Whitsun Wedding' (*CP*114). In his poem 'Going, Going' (*CP* 189), the enemy is the consumers whose kids are screaming 'For more-/More houses, more parking allowed/More caravan sites, more pay' (*CP* 189), and in 'Wants', the enemy is the exploiters who reduce life to a few tableaux of society (invitation cards), and who commercially exploit the natural sexual desires (the printed directions of sex). It is also those people who are 'all of the mind', as simplified in the proud family, which celebrates its union and belonging to the nation under the flag:

Beyond all this, the wish to be alone:
However the sky grows dark with invitation-cards
However we follow the printed directions of sex
However the family is photographed under the flagstaff-
Beyond all this, the wish to be alone. (*CP* 42)

It is this kind of crowd that terrifies Larkin, not 'the British mass society', in general, as Tom Paulin suggests.[14] Almost ten years before his poem 'Wants', which was written in 1950, Larkin wrote a letter to his friend Sutton expressing his distaste for those people who are 'all of the mind': 'Oxford terrified me. Public schoolboys terrified me. The dons terrified me. So did the scouts'.[15] In another letter, dated 1951, he said that 'Glimpses I get of any fixed or corporate life repel me - married life, or family life, or the drunken bourgeois dance at my hotel in Loughborough that made me want to saw people's heads off'. [16]

In 'Wants', Larkin summarizes most of the existential views and thoughts increasingly permeating his poems in a later period, from the mid-sixties onward, especially in his last collection *High Windows* (1974). In this poem, Larkin is neither a disillusioned nor a frustrated poet. Nor is he a poet of restrained emotions, but a poet who feels through the intellect, and expresses his thoughts about society and individuality, about the dominant culture of consumerism, selfhood and otherness.

He generalises his ideas by using the first person plural to suggest that longing for solitude is not a private, but a universal concern. The poet not only invites us to be involved in his feelings, but also to share his decisive conclusions as if they are existential facts, by his use of the first person plural. He often uses this technique when he wants to engage his readers in the poem. In the second stanza of 'Wants', Larkin transcends the poem to a higher level, by replacing the word 'Wish', in the first stanza, by a stronger word 'Desire', in the second stanza, and by shifting from wanting loneliness to passionate yearning for oblivion. He also replaces 'Beyond' by 'Beneath', and uses the verb 'Run', as if urgently driven by the forces of oblivion. There is no 'Freudian death wish' in the second stanza of the poem, as Kuby[17] and John Osborne suggest.[18] Neither is 'Want' an escapist poem, as Booth suggests.[19] The desire for oblivion here is fully conscious and thought out. It is a rejection of a consumer society, which turns time into commercial art (the calendar), life and human fear of death into a profitable trade (the life insurance business):

Beneath it all, desire of oblivion runs:
Despite the artful tensions of the calendar,
The life insurance, the tabled fertility rites,
The costly aversion of the eyes from death –
Beneath it all, desire of oblivion runs. (*CP* 42)

Longing for absence, for solitude, for inwardness versus outwardness, is a main characteristic of the outsider, who always escapes from an outside world perceived as artificial, and hurries to his private space, because 'there seems to be no reason for doing anything else'[20] in a society, whose life is 'immobile, locked', as Larkin says in 'The Life With a Hole in It' (*CP* 202). In this poem,

20

published in 1974, we are presented with the same theme reflected in 'Wants', almost twenty-five years later. It is essentially the same world, in which there is a 'three-handed struggle between our wants and the society', and which loses its human meaning because of the unbeatable slow machine:

Life is an immobile, locked,
Three-handed struggle between
Your wants, the world's for you, and (worse)
The unbeatable slow machine
That brings what you'll get. Blocked,
They strain round a hollow statis
Of havings–to, fear, faces.
Days sift down it constantly. Years (*CP* 202)

The outsiders, in the poetry of Larkin at least, are not neurotic personalities, but are a reaction to the consumer society they inhabit. In this sense, the persona of Mr. Bleaney is a typical outsider. This poem, which is perhaps the most existential poem Larkin ever wrote, depicts a person who has no money, no house, no family and no identity. We only know his surname. He lives in a room which is 'one hired box'. He is locked in this box for a long time until 'curtains flower, thin and frayed/ Fall to within five inches of the sill' (*CP* 102). At last, the landlady removes him. A new tenant moves into the

21

same room and begins to meditate on the existentialist conditions of his predecessor. We see that the new lodger, who is the speaker in the poem, is indeed another version of the old lodger, or Larkin himself, as he points out:

The two-thirds of the poem, down to 'But if', are concerned with my uneasy feeling that I am becoming Mr. Bleaney, yes. The last third is reassuring myself that I am not, because he was clearly quite content with his sauce instead of gravy and digging the garden and so on, and yet there's doubt lingering too, perhaps he hated it as much as I did'.[21]

The use of the technique of disguise, however, helps to transcend the poem from the concrete internal scene of the room to the level of reflection on the human condition. 'Mr. Bleaney' raises two difficult issues that preoccupy existentialists. It is worth noting here that the outsider always 'tends to express himself in existentialist terms'.[22] The first issue is about the freedom of choice, or what Kierkegaard calls, 'the dizziness of freedom',[23] exemplified in questions such as, 'Whether or not Mr. Bleaney is able to detach himself from what seems, to the outsider, a tawdry and futile life?'.[24] The second issue is concerned with consciousness: whether or not Mr. Bleaney is conscious

22

of his condition. The answer of Mr. Bleaney's double, or the poet himself, to these two questions is, 'I don't know' (*CP* 103). This answer endorses, firstly, the existentialist's view that 'our choice is accompanied by Angst at the array of alternative options thereby annulled',[25] and, secondly, it implies uncertainty. The first view is reflected in other poems such as 'The Building', where 'The end of choice, the last of hope', (*CP* 191) in 'To My Wife': 'Choice of you shuts up that peacock-fan' (*CP* 54), and in 'The Old Fools', where the two views are reflected in the second stanza:

… Next time you can't pretend
There'll be anything else. And these are the first signs:
Not knowing how, not hearing who, the power
Of choosing gone. (*CP* 196)

Larkin expresses a similar spirit of existential uncertainty, of 'knowing nothing' in his poem 'Ignorance', which was written in 1955: 'Strange to know nothing, never to be sure/ Of what is true or right or real' (*CP* 107).

In the first line of the last stanza of 'Mr Bleaney', Larkin generalizes the state of Mr. Bleaney. The poem shifts from 'He' in the previous stanzas to 'We' in the first line of the last stanza to lock us, the readers, inside the poem, not only the double, or the poet. He also transcends the whole poem to the level of the abstract in the line: 'That how we live measures our own nature' (*CP* 103), which reminds us of Eliot's Prufrock:

I have measured out my life with coffee spoons;
I know the voices dying with a dying fall
Beneath the music from a farther room
So how should I presume? [26]

In his book *The Society of the Poem*, the British critic Jonathan Raban tries to read 'Mr Bleaney' from both a polyphonic and class angle. He points out that 'Mr. Bleaney' strikes him as 'a remarkably successful example of a poem which is very much like a political democracy of a peculiarly muddled and English kind'.[27] He also argues that the poem is 'multilingual, and each idiom corresponds exactly to a social tone, even if the idioms are defined in rather literary terms: the declassed 'narrator', the proletarian 'character', and the essentially aristocratic voice of poetry'.[28] However, it seems that 'Mr. Bleaney' echoes the French writer Henri Barbusse's novel *L'Enfer*, whose protagonist spends all his time watching the world from a hole in his room like Mr. Bleaney's, who spends the whole time at the Bodies in a room without any space for books or bags, and whose

24

'window shows a strip of building land, tussocky, littered' (*CP* 102).

In his book *The Outsider*, the British writer Colin Wilson argues that what characterises the outsider is a 'sense of strangeness, unreality'. According to him, Camus, Barbusse, and Hemingway have emphasized the practical nature of 'this living problem, the problem of a pattern or purpose in life'. [29]

Larkin expresses this problem of self-realisation in a letter to a friend in the late sixties: 'I am doomed to die without having done anything I pine to do, because the things I want to do are essentially undoable, they belong to the imagination'. In another letter in 1967, he wrote: 'I am growing defeatist. I am not even turning into a regional poet.... Just an anonymous figure, whom people will dimly remember seeing'.[30] In this regard, as the British critic Terry Whalen argues persuasively in his book *Philip Larkin and English Poetry*, Larkin is close to poets such as Ted Hughes, Tom Gunn and R.S. Thomas, who share with them, 'not only the depth and integrity, but also profound doubts, tensions, and existential anxieties, and exploration which are everywhere attentive to bleaker truth and realities of our day'.[31] I would argue that Larkin is closer to R.S. Thomas. It might even be claimed that Larkin shares more themes with Thomas than with any other British poet in the second half of the twentieth century, though their approaches and styles have differences.

Waiting, absences, death, failure, suffering, echo, shadows, and death, are very common vocabularies in their poetic discourse. It seems that both poets echo ideas of Kierkegaard, perhaps unconsciously, in the case of Larkin, and consciously with Thomas, who read Kierkegaard and dedicated a poem to him:

And beyond the window Denmark
Waited, but refused to adopt
This family that wore itself out
On its conscience, up and down in one room.
Meanwhile the acres
Of the imagination grow
Unhindered, though they always paused
At that labourer, the indictment
Of whose gesture was a warped
Crucifix upon a hill
In Jutland. The stern father
Look at it and a hard tear
Formed, that the child's frightened
Sympathy could not convert
To a plaything. [32]

Both poets are preoccupied with almost the same existential themes: outsiderness, freedom of choice, solitude, absence, frustration, misery and spiritual failure in materialistic modern society. Unlike the secular Larkin, Thomas's approaches to his themes are arguably theological, but his main concern, like Larkin, is the human condition. In their lives and works, both poets seek to solve the dichotomy between art and life, between 'two hungers, hunger for bread, and hunger of the uncouth soul for the light's grace', as beautifully expressed by Thomas's poem 'Dark Well'.[33]

For both Larkin and Thomas, the question of belonging is at the core of their existential philosophy, in the broad sense of the word, whether it takes an arguably empirical perspective, as is the case with Larkin, or a theological form as with Thomas. This is evident in many of their poems. In 'Via Negativa', Thomas explores the themes of belonging, dislocation, alienation, and existential anxiety, almost in the same manner as we see in Larkin's above-mentioned poem 'Places, of Loved Ones'. Thomas writes:

Why no!
I never thought other than
That God is that great absence
In our lives, the empty silence

Within, the place where we go
Seeking not in hope to
Arrive or find. [34]

Larkin writes: 'No, I have never found/ The place where
I could say/ This is my proper ground/ Here I shall stay'
(CP 99). If we compare Larkin's 'Church Going' with
Thomas's 'In Church', we can see that both poets raise
essentially the same existential question, though from a
different angle. Thomas writes:

Often I try
To analyse the quality
Of its silences. Is this where God hides
From my searching? I have stopped to listen,
After the few people have gone,
To the air recomposing itself
For vigil.
{…}
Shadows advance
From their corners to take possession
Of places the light held
For an hour. The bats resume
Their business. The uneasiness of the pews
Ceases. There is no other sound
In the darkness but the sound of a man
Breathing, testing his faith

On emptiness, nailing his questions

One by one to an untenanted cross.[35]

Larkin writes:

Once I am sure there's nothing going on

I step inside, letting the door thud shut.

{....}

A shape less recognisable each week,

A purpose more obscure. I wonder who

Will be the last, the very last, to seek

This place for what it was; one of the crew

That tap and jot and know what rood-lofts were?

{....}

It pleases me to stand in silence here. (*CP* 98)

In his book *Out of Reach: The Poetry of Philip Larkin*, Andrew Swarbrick unconvincingly argues that 'the moment of most intense assent in Larkin, his own 'enormous yes', comes with the vocabulary of nullity: nowhere, absences, oblivion {…} the terror of death is matched by the yearning for annihilation'.[36] The poet Charles Tomlinson sees Larkin's poetry as 'the joke which hesitates just on this side of nihilism'.[37] This view is misguided. There are, however, plenty of elements of bleakness in Larkin's poems. In his poem 'An Arundel Tomb', Larkin declares that 'living is a dreadful thing'

(*CP* 240). In 'Poetry of Departure' (*CP* 95), he says: 'we all hate home', or 'Home is sad' (*CP* 119). He also expresses his crisis of self-realization, uncertainty, and his sense of unreality in an 'unfenced existence' (*CP* 37), where he feels it is 'Strange to know nothing, never to be sure/ Of what is true or right or real' (*CP* 107). This unresolved response to existence, and the 'long troubled argument with himself', in the words of Tom Paulin,[38] can be found in most of his poems, but Larkin does not negate or devalue life.

His personae, whether in poetry or prose, are not like Bazarov, the protagonist of the Russian novelist Ivan Turgenev's *Fathers and Children*, the first novel in literature in which the main concern is nihilism. Like Larkin's speaker in 'Wants', Bazarov consistently expresses his desire to be alone. But in Bazarov's case, loneliness leads to nihilism.

Bazarov resorts to the 'reduction of everything men consider 'higher', the things of mind and spirit, to the lower or 'basic': matter, sensation, the physical'. He unequivocally declares that 'most useful of all is negation', and that 'everything must be crushed because truth can not be known', or 'there is no truth at all. The most important thing is that two times two makes four. The rest is nonsense'.[39]

In his book *The End of Modernity*, the Italian author and philosopher Gianni Vattimo identifies Nietzsche's concept of nihilism with this situation of meaningless. For Nietzsche, nihilism is a process in which there is nothing left. Vattimo argues that Nietzsche characterises nihilism as 'emptying the world and especially human existence of meaning, purpose, comprehensible truth, or essential value'. It is 'a will to nothingness, where life turns away from itself, as there is nothing to be found in this world'.[40] As we see in his poetry, Larkin does not seek to negate reality, or even to reconstruct it. He uses his observations of reality to explore ugliness and absurdity in our existence, and to rediscover the aesthetics of life in 'outwardly witnessing poetry which goes past subjectivism in its struggle toward a healing connection with surrounding life'.[41] We can find this 'healing connection with surrounding life' in some of Larkin's poems like 'To the Sea' (*CP*173), and 'The Whitsun Weddings' (*CP*114), where he finds himself among ordinary people.

In 'To the Sea', the poet celebrates everything: crowds under the low horizon, steep beach, blue tower, towels, and red bathing caps (*CP* 173). He celebrates people on the beach because they are ordinary, spontaneous, sympathetic, and as beautiful as nature in the summer.

They are also innocently naked as nature, without any guises to hide their personalities behind. They come to water clumsily undressed year after year, teaching their children, and helping the old too. They are different from those 'drunken bourgeois' who dance at his hotel in Loughborough, and make Larkin want 'to saw people's heads off'. There is harmony in 'To the Sea' between nature, people, things, however trivial they are (Rocks, Soup tins, Pebbles, Cigars...), and the speaker, as if they are one unity. The strong sense of solitude evident in other poems is replaced in this poem by a connection with people and nature. The images of this poem are concrete and sensuous in order to reflect the physicality of the scene, in which the poet involves all the senses in a celebration of beauty. In 'To the Sea', Larkin observes and absorbs what he sees, as he does, for example, in 'The Whitsun Wedding' (*CP* 114).

'To the Sea' is composed of seemingly disconnected matters. But the changing relationships between things reflect directly, and in very direct and prosaic language, the psychological and emotional state of the poet at a specific place and time, between the personal and the general, between past and present, and, most importantly, between place as a physical location and the poet's consciousness and identity. First, the poet feels happy at being on his own (*C P*173), after he crosses the wall which separates the natural world (the sea) from the city, where an artificial life of money and consumption dominates: 'To step over the low wall that divides/ Road from concrete walk above the shore/ Brings sharply back something known long before-/ the miniature gaiety of seasides' (*CP*173). The poet seems to be very sensitive to his own presence, and gradually feelings of strangeness and loneliness are replaced with a strong sense of belonging, as he gradually becomes part of the scene, and falls in love with the ordinary:

As when, happy at being on my own,
I searched the sand for Famous Cricketers,
Or, farther back, my parents, listeners
To the same seaside quack, first became known.
Strange to it now, I watch the cloudless scene:
The same clear water over smoothed pebbles,
The distant bathers' weak protesting trebles
Down at its edge, and then the cheap cigars,
The chocolate-papers, tea-leaves, and, between
The rocks, the rusting soup-tins, till the first
Few families start the trek back to the cars. (*CP* 173)

Again, there are no metaphors in this poem. The poet describes real things in a specific place, in scenes which are almost photographic (cheap cigars, chocolate-papers, tea–leaves, …). The whole movement makes the scene, the people, the poet, and the readers inhabit the poem, through transcending the lived experience to the level of the conceptual, and thus leading us to imaginatively enter into another world, far away from the bleak world. As in 'To the Sea', we are presented in 'the Whitsun Weddings' (*CP* 114) with the speaker's celebration of human beauty. Larkin explains in an interview that the poem arose from a railway journey between Hull and London on Whit Saturday, 1955.[42] The train stops at every station, but Larkin does not realize that it 'was the train that all wedding couples would get on and go to London for their honeymoons'.[43] We see that the speaker in the first two stanzas is an outsider:

At first, I didn't notice what a noise
The Weddings made
Each station that we stopped at: sun destroys
The interest of what's happening in the shade,
And down the long cool platforms whoops and skirls
I took for porters larking with the mails,
And went on reading…. (*CP* 114).

At first, the scene looks very gloomy: 'All windows down, all cushions hot' (*CP* 114). The things outside are not more pleasant: 'We ran/ Behind the backs of houses,

34

crossed a street / Of blinding windscreens, smelt the fish dock; ...'. There are also 'Canals with floatings of industrial froth; / A hothouse flashed uniquely: hedges dipped/ and rose: ...'. The poet is still an outsider, but from the third stanza, there is a big shift in the speaker's mood, from aloneness to involvement. The poet has become part of the scene with all his senses: he sees, hears and smells. The poet also involves us by replacing 'I' by 'We'. The personal experience becomes a shared experience. Now there is interaction and interrelationship between the personal and the general. Feelings of strangeness and foreignness, reflected in most of Larkin's poems, are replaced with a strong sense of belonging. Solitude melts into participation.

In her book *An Uncommon Poet For The Common Man*, Kuby argues that the train ride is a metaphor for life, and the train is a vehicle of destiny carrying its passengers to their fate.[44] Quite the reverse. The train ride, the vehicle, the passengers are real things with an independent existence. They are also real inside the framework of the poem, not metaphors for anything outside. Larkin writes the following about this shared emotional experience between him and the passengers:

... train that stopped at every station and I hadn't realized that, of course, this was the train that all the wedding couples would get on and go to London for their honeymoon. {....} They all looked different but they were all doing the same things and sort of feeling the same thing. {....} Every time you stopped fresh emotion climbed aboard. And finally between Peterborough and London when you hurtled on, you felt the whole thing was being aimed like a bullet-at the heart of things, you know. All this fresh open life. Incredible experience. I've never forgotten it. [45]

Chapter 2

Transcending sex

Though 'High Windows' (*CP* 165), the title poem of the collection of the same name, consists of only five short stanzas, it is one of Philip Larkin's most important poems. It is important for Larkin's poetry because it summarizes in a few lines some of the themes that preoccupied Larkin as a poet and as a human being: namely his seemingly contradictory views on love, sex, age, solitude and deprivation. The poem moves between the ordinary and the sublime, between the general and the personal, between the present and the past, and between the physical and the conceptual, and sometimes does so within the one stanza, as do many of Larkin's mature poems from the mid-sixties on. The first stanza comes across as sensuous and colloquial, 'taking on the aura of somebody's thought that might be part of conversation in the pub'.[1] The language is simple and direct. This is in sharp contrast to the suggestive language of the following stanzas, as we will see. On the surface level, this stanza does not seem part of the poem psychologically or conceptually, but a separate piece with its own style of prose, as if it stands on its own with its decisive, authoritative judgment in the last line:

When I see a couple of kids
And guess he's fucking her and she
Taking pills or wearing a diaphragm,
I know this is paradise (*CP* 165).

By this judgment, Larkin seems to do away with 'three quarters of the enjoyment which derived from the satisfaction of guessing the poem little by little'.[2] He leaves nothing for our imagination to guess about. But the poet consciously misleads the reader making him enter the world of the poem to experience what the poet has experienced and accordingly, receive a different message. The line 'I know this is paradise' is clever and ironic. It seems to be an authoritative judgment, but we will discover in the following stanzas that this impression is false. A technique similar to that used in the collection of the same name, *High Windows,* is being employed and it draws on the influence of the symbolist movement. In this collection, the symbolist device helps him 'disrupt the normal relationships between concepts, and, by liberating him from the familiar, circumscribed world, it allows him to experience and convoy a sense of transcendence'.[3] This process of transcendence is achieved not through creating ambivalent elements within the syntax of the poem to reach a state of synthesis, as in the case of Yeats, but through a process of meditation, like Thomas Hardy. There is almost no single idea to be developed throughout the poem, but the meaning penetrates the whole poem, or may be accumulated in its final stanza. This style has become characteristic of his collection *High Windows*, published in 1974, ten years after the success of *The Whitsun Wedding*, under the influence of Hardy, who helped him 'shake off the heady fumes of Yeatsian rhetoric'.[4]

This style, however, has a strong tradition in English poetry. In her comprehensive book *An Uncommon Poet For The Common Man*, Canadian critic and poet Lolette Kuby goes back to the sixteenth century to argue that Larkin's difference from his contemporaries resembles Ben Jonson's differences from his contemporaries in many respects:

Both tend to avoid extended metaphor, strings of similes, and other rhetorical elaborations, which, in Jonson's time, were called 'conceits', or 'bravery' of language {...} Both express themselves succinctly, attempting, as Jonson put it, 'what man can say / In a little', the poetic impulse being toward reduction and condensation rather than expansion and extension.

Neither depends on single, striking lines and memorable phrases to carry the meaning.[5]

Other critics, like Motion, think that such style 'feeds into him from - among others - Wordsworth, Tennyson, Hardy, Edward Thomas, A.E. Houseman and Auden'.[6] It also nourishes, according to Motion, a large number of other recent poets who have not been associated with the Movement, particularly John Betjeman, whom Larkin admired. In the second stanza of 'High Windows', the poem transcends the concreteness of the first stanza, the act of love, to the level of the conceptual (Everyone old has dreamed of all their lives), from the act of seeing to the field of imagination, from the personal (When I see) to the general (Everyone old):

Everyone old has dreamed of all their lives-
Bonds and gestures pushed to one side
Like an outdated combine harvester,
And everyone young going down the long slide.
To happiness, endlessly. {...} (*CP* 165)

On the surface, it seems that the old, who have dreamed all their lives of sexual freedom, envy the young generation who have been freed from sexual taboos by the sexual revolution which had spread throughout the Western societies from the early 1960s. (The poem was written in 1967). But the poet, consciously or unconsciously, deceives us once again leading to corresponding misinterpretations like those by Petch and Motion. In his book *The Art of Philip Larkin*, Simon Petch argues that the poet's own feelings about youth's freedom from sexual inhibitions are not essentially different from the way his elders used to imagine his freedom from religious inhibitions. Thus, the poet, according to him, has imagined two sets of attitudes, and let them collapse. It is a freedom from the ordinary world, and also from the uneasy sense of not belonging to the ordinary world.[7] Motion also suggests that Larkin realizes, as he speculates about the new generation's chances of happiness, that he might have been similarly envied. He goes on to say:

The poem grows out of rage: the rage of unsatisfied desire, the rage of 'shame', the rage of having to persuade everyone that 'the thought of high windows' guarantees happiness. The poem's beautifully achieved shift from the empirical to the symbolic cannot disguise or subdue Larkin's appetite for what he has never had.[8]

That is simply not true. In his poem 'Annus Mirabilis', Larkin confesses that his sexual intercourse began in 1963. At that time he was 41:

Sexual intercourse began

In nineteen sixty-three
(Which was rather late for me)-
Between the end of the *Chatterley* ban
And the Beatles' first LP. (*CP* 167)

In an early letter to his friend Jim Sutton, Larkin writes: 'sex is designed for people who like overcoming obstacles. I don't like overcoming obstacles.'[9] Another friend recalls him saying things like 'Oh I wish you could get sex and pay for it monthly like you do the laundry, because it's all so difficult'.[10] M.W. Rowe, and other critics, like Janice Rossen, suggest that Larkin had difficulties with women due partly to his ugliness. Rowe also believes that Larkin had a low opinion of himself inherited from his father, while others accuse him of being a misogynist. The reason runs much deeper. Larkin's views about women are part of his larger struggle with life, as an outsider. Like any outsider, Larkin, or the persona in 'High Windows' at least, is indecisive man. The outsider believes that 'nothing is worth doing, no way is better than the other',[11] or 'It is not worth doing anything'.[12] He just watches life passing before him. He does not act, because any act may face obstacles, and 'he does not like overcoming obstacles', as Larkin says. Outsider personalities 'can never do anything other than react to other people'.[13] The persona in 'The Love Song of J. Alfred Prufrock', by T.S. Eliot is an ideal example of such a personality. Every act for Prufrock, even eating a peach, seems to be an obstacle to overcome. He always needs time to meditate on whether to do or not to do something, no matter how trivial, and he self-deceptively thinks that there will always be enough time to make a decision later. It is a kind of social and psychological paralysis:

And indeed there will be time
To wonder' 'Do I dare' and, 'Do I dare?'
Time to turn back and descend the stair,
With a bald spot in the middle of my hair-
(They will say: 'How his hair is growing thin!')
{...}
Shall I part my hair behind? Do I dare to eat a peach?
I shall wear white flannel trousers, and walk upon the beach.
I have heard the mermaids singing, each to each.
I do not think that they will sing to me. [14]

In *The Oxford Book of Twentieth–Century English Verse*, Larkin chose 'The Love Song of J.Alfred Prufrock' to be the first poem to represent T.S. Eliot, alongside 'La Figlia Che Piange', 'Sweeney Erect', 'The Waste Land', 'Journey of the Magi', 'Choruses From Murder in the Cathedral', 'Gus: The Theatre Cat', and 'Little Gidding'.[15] These poems cover thirty pages, while Larkin gives Hardy twenty-six pages, and Yeats eighteen pages. In a 1964 interview with Ian Hamilton, Larkin criticized Eliot and Pound, and 'anybody who is normally regarded modern', but he also acknowledged in the same interview that 'Eliot, like Yeats, had a demonstrable effect on the course of English poetry'.[16] However, Eliot's effect on Larkin's own work can only be recognized in some early poems like 'Wants' (*CP* 42), as mentioned in chapter 1, and 'most of the parallels that have been drawn between Larkin and Eliot concern the resemblance that Larkin's self-deprecating speakers bear to Prufrock'.[17]

In the second stanza of 'High Windows', the ambiguous simile 'Like an outdated combine harvester' refers to something beyond the naïve idea of envy. But to give a convincing explanation of this ambiguity, we have to think of it in its relationship to the whole poem, not to the other lines in the stanza, which spills into the third and fourth stanzas, where

No God any more, or sweating in the dark
About hell and that, or having to hide
What you think of priest. He
And his lot will all go down the long slide
Like free bloody birds. (*CP* 165).

44

It seems here that 'Like an outdated combine harvester' stands on its own, and disrupts the development of ideas in the stanza. Is there a manipulation of language? Or is there a hidden image, as Motion suggests?[18]

We notice in this stanza that there is a shift from the first-person voice in the first stanza (I see/ I know) to the third person. The 'I', of course, is very close to the author, but Larkin soon shifts from the 'I' to the 'He' to dramatize the whole experience of the poem, and to make its perspective seem more objective.

He hides himself behind his protective screen to generalize his thought, which will come suddenly in the third stanza, that neither the young nor the old 'get their oats', because the combine harvester is outdated. Though this line, or the hidden image of it, seems to contrast with the remainder of the same stanza, it is very crucial to understand the third stanza, as Larkin prepares the reader for the last movement of the poem:

….. . And immediately
Rather than words comes the thought of high windows:

The sun-comprehending glass,
And beyond it, the deep blue air, that shows
Nothing, and is nowhere, and is endless. (*CP* 165).

45

Some critics, like A. T. Tolley, think that the relationship of this stanza to the remainder of the poem is elusive even though the ecclesiastical association of 'High windows' reaches back to the reference to 'sweating in the dark/about hell'. Tolley concludes that the experience of the poem, as a whole, 'is not effectively brought into focus'.[19] In his book *Philip Larkin: The Poems*, Nicholas Marsh argues that the link 'And immediately / Rather than words comes the thought' tells us nothing. He goes on to say:

The determinedly colloquial tone of the first four stanzas, and the extreme contrast between this and the final stanza's metaphorical rhetoric, is so surprising that it provokes the question: why? How can a poem move from the awkward earthiness of 'And guess he is fucking her and 'She's taking pills', to the beautiful extended stresses of 'deep blue air', or the perfect tripled cadence of 'Nothing, and is nowhere, and is endless'?[20]

He concludes that the aim of the poem is to 'enact the mismatch between human life and the universe it inhabits'. These unconvincing interpretations emerge, perhaps, from the confusing technique that Larkin adopts in his collection *High Windows*, as mentioned before.

Tolley and Marsh read the poem 'High Windows' as separate stanzas, each of them carrying a meaning, or they read it as if it is built from disconnected elements, not as a unity. Technically, 'High Windows' is divided into five stanzas, but, artistically, it is one piece of meditation on sex, happiness, time and age. It moves between the ordinary and the concrete, the act of sex between a couple of teenagers, and the abstract (the thought of high windows). It also moves between the present and the past. There is no dialectical process which could unify the elements of the poem, but a circular movement, and the poet succeeds in the last stanza in uniting those opposing elements of the poem in one movement through transcending them to the level of the sublime, not through 'dislocating the precise relationship between a concept and a thing', as Motion suggests:[21]

Rather than words comes the thought of high windows:

The sun-comprehending glass,
And beyond it, the deep blue air, that shows
Nothing, and is nowhere, and is endless. (*CP* 165)

The sublimity symbolized in the intensive images of 'thought of high windows', and 'the deep blue air', cannot be expressed because 'it refers to a moment

47

when the ability to apprehend, know, and express a thought or sensation is defeated. Yet, through this very defeat, the mind gets a feeling for what lies beyond thought and language'.[22] For Kant, the sublime is divided into two kinds, the first of which he calls the dynamic sublime. By this, he means that 'we contemplate awesome power, aware that it could easily bring about our own destruction'.[23] But 'although we realise that these forces could destroy our body, we simultaneously realize that there are faculties in us which these forces cannot destroy, namely our forces of practical reason and freedom of the will'.[24] The second kind of sublime is 'mathematical sublime, which arises when we contemplate something vast and try to take it in as a whole'.[25] We can find both kinds of sublime in the poetry of Larkin. Poems like 'Here' and 'Absences' are typical examples of the first kind, while 'High Windows' is a clear case of the second kind, where the sublime arises and takes everything as a whole (The young and the old, and the poet and the reader, the sun-comprehending glass, and the blue air) to a higher level.

Since the mid-sixties, after the publication of his collection *The Whitsun Weddings* in 1964, Larkin sought to write 'different kinds of poems that might be by different people', expressing scepticism of the notion

48

that a poet's work necessarily develops towards a mature stage, an idea which first arose in relation to Yeats' work, according to Larkin. Larkin succeeds in creating different kinds of poems in his collection *High Windows*. In many poems in the collection, and the title-poem 'High Windows' is a good example, we do not see visual imagery or hear rhetorical sentences. In 'High Windows', we see that there are only two similes: 'Like an outdated combine harvester', in the second stanza, and 'like free bloody birds', in the fourth stanza. It is also without metaphors. We can say that the whole poem works as a metaphor, with a layer of meaning developing in parallel to the apparent one.

Chapter 3

Transcending the ordinary

In his recording of The 'Whitsun Weddings',[1] Larkin claims never to have written a poem (with the exception of 'Faith Healing') about a situation that he has not experienced at first hand. He also believes, as he writes in *Required Writing*, that 'poetry is an affair of sanity, of seeing things as they are', and 'should be understood first go', as is the case with the work of John Betjeman, who 'restored direct intelligible communication', and that of Thomas Hardy, whose 'strength is his simplicity'.[2]

He read Hardy with a sense of relief, as he points out: 'I did not have to jack up to a concept of poetry that lay outside my own life, and this is perhaps what I felt Yeats was trying to make me do'.[3] Larkin also attacks professional readers, the dons and their students, and a concept of poetry, which lies outside his own and other people's lives.[4] He expresses his distaste for modernist poetry for the same reasons that make him prefer Hardy over Yeats 'because modernist poetry takes us away from life as we know it'.[5] He confirms these ideas in an interview with the poet Ian Hamilton:

What I do feel a bit rebellious about is that poetry seems to have got into the hands of a critical industry which is concerned with culture in the abstract, and this I do rather lay at the door of Eliot or Pound. {…} I think a lot of the 'myth-kitty business' has grown out of that, because first of all you have to be terribly educated, you have to read everything to know these things, and secondly, you've got somehow to work them in to show that you are working them in. But to me the whole of the ancient world, the whole of classical and biblical mythology means very little, and I think that using them today not only fills poems full of dead spots but dodges the writer's duty to be original.[6]

Larkin went to some pains to project himself as a simple, anti-intellectual poet, and many of his critics concur in their assessment of the poems. Let's have some examples. Graham Holderness regards his poetry as 'a poetry of simplicity'. Thus, he concludes that Larkin 'is content to accept and imitate the surface of life, unwilling to drive deeper into systematic thought or into new structures of language; unwilling to explore the depths and complexities of experience or of words'.[7] While Whalen argues that Larkin is 'a poet of immediacy', he paradoxically attributes some vague metaphysical elements to his poetry, which, according to him, 'betrays beauty as a transient wonder at the mystery of the living wonder'.[8] Germaine Greer, who strongly attacked Larkin after the publication of *Selected Letters*, regards Larkin's verse as 'simple, demotic, colloquial' and the attitudes it expresses as 'anti-intellectual, racist, sexist, and rotten class-consciousness'.[9] For critic James Wood, Larkin is 'a minor registrar of disappointment, bureaucrat of frustration', while both writer Bryan Appleyard and poet and critic Peter Ackroyd regard him as a provincial poet.[10] On his part, poet and critic Andrew Duncan writes that Larkin is 'depressing, frigid, boring, had no literary talent, and never managed to write a good poem'.[11]

Larkin's poetry indeed seems simple on the surface, and can be understood 'first go', because he portrays the ordinary in direct and colloquial language, the language of the people. But a careful reading of his poetry reveals that it is no less 'intellectual' and sophisticated than that of Eliot or Pound. Larkin's mature poetry operates at a profound level, and reflects the basic existential questions which preoccupied humanity in the twentieth century. But in contrast to Pound and Eliot, Larkin's sophistication does not grow out of 'myth-kitty business', to use Larkin's own term, or out of philosophical meditation on contemporary civilization and human conditions, but firstly from his technique, of which Auden was a known admirer,[12] and, secondly, from his sophisticated process of recreating the ordinary, which we will examine more closely later. In most of his mature poems, Larkin constructs new relationships between disparate things and language using the syntax of the poem itself, where he 'often makes it do what he wants to do', as Eliot once said about Larkin's poetry.[13]

But the success of such a process depends on the technique that the poet employs. In most of his mature poems, Larkin recreates ordinary things in order to give them a meaning which differs from the commonplace meaning. They are no longer things per se. They lose their autonomy when they are put into relation with each other, and acquire new meanings within the landscape of the poem, as we see, for example in the poem 'Water':

If I were called in
To construct a religion
I should make use of water
{....}

And I should raise in the east
A glass of water
where any-angled light
Would congregate endlessly. (*CP* 93)

This poetic power of transcending physical things can be traced through many of Larkin's mature poems. In 'The Whitsun Weddings', we see 'an arrow-shower' becoming rain somewhere, and in 'Two portraits of Sex' (*CP* 36), many rains and many rivers make one river, and the leaf becomes silver, and the flesh turns gold in 'Deep Analysis' (*CP* 12).

It is true that there is a deep openness to environment in Larkin's poetry, and most of his poems are deeply rooted in reality, but his poetic project is not directed toward discovering the unlimited possibilities of the physical reality before our minds and eyes, as with the New York School poets, for example, nor to make reality more beautiful, or lament missing values like the platonic or idealist poets.

He is a very realist poet, in the sense that his poetic materials are derived from reality, not from ideas. But he does not treat these materials as they are, for their own sake, but instead there is a continuous process of recreating the materials he consciously accumulates in his poems in order to create another reality through the process of transcendence. For this reason, we feel that there is something else that emerges in his poems from the original material, and 'floats free', in Motion's term,[14] creating a state of meditation which seems to function metonymically. Larkin uses different tactics to achieve such transcendence.

In his poem 'Absences' (*CP* 49) written in 1950, Larkin employs a poetic technique of transcendence different from that used in 'High Windows' and 'Here' to transcend the physical materials of his poem. In 'High Windows', as mentioned above, the poet makes an unexpected shift in the narrative of the poem. He moves from a sensuous simile in the last line of the fourth stanza (Like free bloody birds) to a more abstract level in the next stanza (The thought of high windows). He does this without making any poetic preparation for such a big shift. He isolates the final two stanzas from the first three by using the adverb (immediately) to transform the poem to a higher level. In 'Absences', the poet accumulates his materials and places them in scenes which have an almost cinematic quality, as he does in 'Here'. He describes real things in a specific place, and it seems that there is a powerful sense of physical reality:

Rain patters on a sea that tilts and sighs.

Fast-running floors, collapsing into hollows,
Tower suddenly, spray-haired. Contrariwise,
A wave drops like a wall: another follows,
Wilting and scrambling, tirelessly at play
Where there are no ships and no shallows. (*CP* 49)

In contrast to the technique used in 'High Windows', Larkin gradually transcends the materials of 'Absences' to the abstract without surprising us. He prepares himself and the reader from the beginning. From the first line of the second stanza, the poem begins a transformation from both the visual experience of the poet and the physical reality of the scene (the sea) to the level of conceptualisation of place (above the sea) before it reaches its climax of transcendence in the last line of the stanza (Such attics cleared of me! Such absences!). We feel here that the poem has become an explicit process of imagining another place, as Larkin puts it: 'I am always thrilled by the thought of what places look like when I am not there'.[15] The poem 'Absences' opens before us infinite possibilities and alternatives, particularly in its closing line:

Above the sea, the yet more shoreless day,
Riddled by wind, trails lit-up galleries:
They shift to giant ribbing, sift away.
Such attics cleared of me! Such absences! (*CP* 49)

Larkin himself admired this poem, and said that 'it sounds like a different, better poet rather than myself. The last line, for instance, sounds like a slightly-unconvincing translation from a French symbolist. I wish I could write like this more often'.[16] In *A Writer's Life*, Andrew Motion refers just to 'French sources', when he refers to two poems Larkin wrote late 1950 after his move to Belfast: 'In two poems he wrote before the end of the year, 'Absences' and the unpublished 'Verlaine', he adapted French sources'.[15] For Graham Chesters, it, at most, echoes seascapes found in Baudelaire ('Le Voyage'), Rimbaud ('Le Bateau ivre', 'Movement') and Valéry ('Le Cimetière marin'). He goes on to say that the 'last line of 'Absences' might have been provoked by structural similarities with the last, isolated line of Gautier's 'Terza Rima: Sublime aveuglement! magnifique défaut!' This latter poem is anthologized by Berthon in *Nine French Poets*, a text which was part of Larkin's extensive reading in his early months in Belfast.[16]

However, we can notice an echo of French symbolist poet Stephane Mallarmé's technique of 'Pure Sound' in 'Absences'. In the first stanza, there are sounds of the sea, fast-running floors, waves tirelessly at play, and all intermingled with the sound of the wind and the rain.

The internal rhythm (wilting, scrambling), and the alliteration (ships, shallows, shift, sift) add an additional powerful effect to the accelerated rhythm of the poem. In contrast to most of his poems, especially those in the collection *High Windows*, 'Absences' is crowded with metaphors. There is also a dialectical movement between the scene he is meditating upon and the attics he has left behind, then the poem goes back to the sea, and from the sea to an absolute state of absence.

All these factors play an important role in the process of transcendence. Booth rightly argues that the seascape is awe-inspiring because it has been cleared of the poet's emotional lumber and personal resentment. He goes on to say that the genre to which this poem best conforms is a surprising choice for Larkin: the sublime ode. But he unconvincingly regards this sublime as negative because 'the poet seeks no transcendence himself. Rather he remains passive while the seascape transcends him'.[17]

In his book *The Poetry of Philip Larkin*, Swarbrick approves this argument by quoting it as it is.[18] Neither critic provides any explanation for such an interpretation. The transcendence in 'Absences', as in 'Whitsun Weddings', and 'To the Sea', for example, is deliberate. We see that the narrator in 'Absences' does not dissolve on the surface of the poem, or into the scene he contemplates, as in the two poems mentioned before. There is also no process of recreating here, as we see in 'Water' (*CP* 93), or 'Deep Analysis' (*CP* 12). The poet watches a rough sea, describes what he sees, meditates on the awesome landscape, and finally and consciously takes his stance: 'Such attics cleared of me! Such absences' (*CP* 49)! Rarely do we find such an example of freedom of choice in the poetry of Larkin as in 'Absences'.

In the last line quoted above, there is a powerful will to get rid of old realities that the narrator has left behind (represented by the attics), but which still haunt him as he contemplates new realities before the seascape. Here the process of transcendence to reach a state of the sublime is 'negative, but dynamic', to use Kant's term.[19] Despite the fast–running floors, rain pattering, high wind, awesomeness of the sea, he chooses his freedom, and finds great enjoyment in this choice. Larkin seeks, as an outsider, to build an imaginative alternative to a world he does not belong to, to find his 'proper place' and environment. Larkin's poetry is not just a poetry of observation like that of his American contemporaries of the New York School who sought to draw on and perpetuate a modern poetry of observation developed by

Williams Carlos William and whose main preoccupations were 'to capture the everyday events, to write poetry that reflects the world as they experience it in their poetic attempts to dismantle the boundaries between art and life, and explore the possible relations between poetry and quotidian objects, which we often exclude from our sense of self identity, and are not integral to a concept of art. [20]

In contrast to the poetry of the New York School, Larkin's poetry is a poetry of defamiliarization.

As mentioned before, Larkin is a good observer, like any outsider, but he has an exceptional ability to defamiliarize what he observes. But such a process demands a high degree of attentiveness from the poet, as the American critic Marjorie Perloff argues in her pioneering book, *Frank O'Hara*: *Poet Among Painters* where she writes 'Art defamiliarizes objects by presenting them as if seen for the first time, or by distorting their forms {...} In his drive to ''defamiliarize'' the ordinary, the artist must be as attentive as possible to the world around him'.[21] But attentiveness alone is not sufficient to achieve the process of defamiliarization. The French philosopher Maurice Merleau-Ponty suggests in his book *The Primary of Perception*, that attention in itself does not create any perception. It is a projective activity, which develops sensory data beyond their own specific significance.[22] For him, 'the evidence of the perceived thing lies in its concrete aspect, in the very texture of its qualities, and in equivalence among all its sensible properties'.[23] The significant difference between the New York School lies in the fact that behind the seeming simplicity of Larkin's poetry, there is a conscious discourse, which explores, recreates, and defamiliarizes the ordinary, whereas the main poetic purpose of New York School poets is to celebrate the ordinary as it is, and thus help us understand the significance of the familiar by presenting it as if seen for the first time. We see this, for example, in the poetry of Frank O'Hara:

Oh! Kangaroos, sequins, chocolate sodas!
You really are beautiful! Pearls
Harmonicas, jujubes, aspirins! all
The stuff they've always talked about
Still makes a poem surprise!
These things are with us every day
Even on beachheads and biers. They
Do have meaning. They're strong as rocks. [24]

Larkin once wrote that 'Betjeman, in a time of global concepts, insisted on the little, the forgotten, the unprofitable, the obscure'.[25]

Larkin's poem 'Here' (*CP* 136) is itself a perfect example of how he described Betjeman's poetry, although perhaps in a more sophisticated style which allows for opposing interpretations.

In 'Here' Larkin focuses on the little and the forgotten, but unlike Betjeman, he strips them from their social, psychological contexts and also from their physicality and immediacy in order to transcend them to the level of the abstract. In this way, he makes a shift in our perception of reality, and, consequently, in our views of our lives and existence. Though 'Here' was written in 1961, 'when the consumer revolution was well underway, and export targets had been achieved, employment levels were high and credit was widely available for the purchase of consumer goods',[26] we are presented in the first stanza with contemporary post-war England simplified in many images in the first stanza: huge industrial buildings (rich industrial shadows), gloomy traffic, the river's slow presence, thin and thistled fields, and the immobile workmen.

In the first stanza, the poet assembles seemingly disparate materials: industrial shadows, traffic, fields, meadows, workmen, scarecrows, haystacks, hares, peasants, a river, clouds, and mud. He seems very distant from the scene he is describing. Furthermore, we do not know from what vantage point he is observing the materials of the poem. Tolley argues that the poem seems to arise from the experience of travelling. He suggests that the train sets the speaker down in Hull, where 'the working day is beginning',[27] while Roger Day argues that 'and now and then a harsh named halt' is 'a reference to rail halts',[28] and James Booth writes that the poem 'begins in the physical separateness of a train'.[29]

In his book *Philip Larkin: Art and Self*, M.W. Rowe argues against the rail hypothesis. He concludes, however, that the poet allows his imaginary point of view to travel through a familiar town (Hull) and countryside, and this does not require him to imagine a method of transport.[30] The title of the poem is also problematic. Rowe sees two difficulties in this regard. First, we have no gestures to guide us, and, secondly, the narrator so obviously moves. He dedicates seven pages of his book to examining the possible meanings of the title, whether it refers to Hull, England, or, in a broader context, the earthly existence, the very state of being alive'.[31] Simon Petch agrees that the poem 'shows us contemporary England'[32] while Osborne writes that the poem 'swings towards, through and then out the other side of Kingston upon Hull in a continuous cinematic panning action that moves ceaselessly forward until the land and the world give out'.[33] He also notes that the poem pauses in Hull, where Larkin died. Because of the repetitious syntax of 'Here', he suggests that the poem might more fittingly be retitled 'Here and now Here and now Here and now Here and now Here'.[34]

In 'Here', Larkin employs two tactics to transcend this poem. The first is used in 'To the Sea' (*CP* 173) and 'The Whitsun Weddings' (*CP* 114), where he accumulates disconnected things before reaching the state of transcendence. It is similar to Eliot's tactic of 'mixing and matching', used particularly in 'The Waste Land' to reach a state of transcendence. Larkin only uses this technique in the first three of the four stanzas of this poem, each of eight lines. In 'High Windows' (*CP* 165) as mentioned above, the poet separates the last stanza from the other stanzas to transcend the poem, and uses only the last line in 'Absences' (*CP* 49) to transcend it. 'Here' opens with 'Swerving east', followed by an accumulation of materials (industrial shadows, traffic, fields, meadows, workmen), but unexpectedly the poet breaks from the narrative, making a shift in the fifth line from flows of concrete images to an isolated abstract statement (swerving to solitude), thus uncovering the poetic purpose of the poem, and leaving nothing for our imaginations to guess at, which relatively 'wanes the effects', of the poem, to use the term of Fredric Jameson.[35] Or does the poet deliberately prepare us from the beginning for the shift to transcendence which will occur in the last stanza? But what does 'Swerving east' refer to? Who is swerving east, then to solitude?

There is no 'I' here dissolving in the materials the poet contemplates, as we see in 'The Whitsun Weddings' (*CP* 114), and 'To the Sea' (*CP* 173), where the 'I' sees, hears, feels, participates and articulates statements or meditations. We do not know who watches, and narrates the story. Nor do we know to what place the title 'Here' refers. Is the whole poem a kind of transcended state, in which people, animals, and things are just shadows in an 'unfenced existence' (*CP* 137), which is 'out of reach' (*CP* 137), and cannot be materialized in a proper grammatical syntax? Swarbrick writes that 'Larkin, in a remarkable feat of syntactical control, makes the first sentence last twenty-four lines, and its suspended present participle, 'Swerving', which anticipates a subject, actually turns out itself to be the subject of the main verb 'Gathers',[36] which is the first word in the second stanza. Rowe argues that 'Gathers itself is clearly a metaphor, and therefore 'Swerving east' can only be the grammatical subject of the metaphor if it is construed metaphorically'.[37] He points out, however, that Larkin's strategy of hiding the subject is extremely risky, and that Larkin was aware of these problems and their obvious solutions, and 'this suggests that the poem's elusive grammar is deliberate; indeed, that it is an essential part of its meaning and effect'.[38]

He is right, but the reasons behind Larkin's strategy of hiding the subject, I would argue, are different from the three points Rowe suggests. The first he mentions is that 'it's a wonderful way to emphasize speed'. The second is that 'everything about the poem is unstable; all its main structural features (its title, narration, genre etc.) balance on the edge of undecidability. He concludes that the elusive nature of the grammatical subject is simply of a piece with these larger difficulties. Larkin in 'Here' deliberately deprives the language of its logic, and does not give it a reasonable syntax, in order to alienate it in accordance with the absurd world he depicts in the poem. Not only is there no subject, but also not a single full stop until the end of the final stanza, as though to suggest that swerving to solitude, to a world out of reach, is an indefinite process.

We have good reason to conclude here that the whole poem has been transcended from the beginning, starting with the title, and the deliberate use of 'Swerving to solitude' at the start of the first stanza. It is deliberately an abstract poem, in the sense that it is not about a specific place, whether that be Hull or England. It is also not about a specific time. It is about all places and times. This is evident in the movement of the poem between the past and present, and between the old and new history of human beings, though Larkin uses only the present tense in 'Here', to suggest that the past is still present in our modern times. In the first stanza, as Rowe notes, all-night traffic could only have been found in the twentieth century, the halts could have been found during and after the nineteenth, but the scarecrows and haystacks could have been found in medieval times'.[39] In this sense, the unmentioned subject could be the absolute 'we', who are swerving to solitude far away from the industrial cities and our modern world, which has turned to become an omnipresent market of selling and buying that does not spare even the dead:

Gathers to the surprise of a large town:
Here domes and statues, spires and cranes cluster

Beside grain-scattered streets, barge-crowded water,
And residents from raw estates, brought down
The dead straight miles by stealing flat-faced trolleys.
(*CP* 136)

In the following two stanzas, Larkin continues his observation and process of accumulation of disparate things (cheap suits, red kitchen-ware, sharp shoes, iced lollies, electric mixers, toasters, washers, driers), mixing them with people (a cut price crowd, salesmen, tattoo-shop owners, grim head-scarfed wives), and nature as well (Fast-shadowed wheat fields, hedges).

All inhabit the poem to be transcended in the final stanza beyond the 'isolate villages, where removed lives/ Loneliness clarifies', where

...... silence stands
Like heat. Here leaves unnoticed thicken,
Hidden weeds flower, neglected waters quicken,
Luminously-peopled air ascends.
And past the poppies bluish neutral distance
Ends the land suddenly beyond a beach
Of shapes and shingle. Here is unfenced existence:
Facing the sun, untalkative, out of reach. (*CP* 136-137)

This conclusion is neither an escape from loneliness, as Tolley[40] and Swarbrick[41] suggest, nor a yearning for 'absolute, unattainable emptiness', as Rossen argues.[42]

These concluding lines 'constitute an epiphany, an escape from the "scrupulous meanness" of the disillusioned intelligence', as Heaney rightly points out. He goes on to say that 'we need only compare 'Here' with 'Show Saturday', another poem that seeks its form by accumulation of details, to see how vital to the success of 'Here' is this gesture towards a realm beyond the social and historical'.[43]

Notes

Introduction

[1] Philip Larkin, *Further Requirements*, ed. by Anthony Thwaite (London: Faber and Faber, 2002), p. 37.

[2] Larkin, *Further Requirements*, p.37.

Chapter 1:   Transcending solitude

[1] Janice Rossen, 'Difficulties with Girls' in *Philip Larkin*, ed. by Stephen Regan (London: Macmillan, 1997), 138), pp. 135- 159, (p. 138).

[2] Philip Larkin, *Collected Poems*, ed. by Anthony Thwaite (London: Faber and Faber, 1988), p. 33.

[3] Larkin, qtd in, *New Larkins for Old*, ed. by James Booth (London: Palgrave, 2000), p.113.

[4] Philip Larkin, *Jill* (London: Faber and Faber), 2005.

[5] *Philip Larkin, A Girl in Winter* (London: Faber and Faber), 1975.

[6] Liz Hedgecock, in *New Larkins For Old*, pp. 97-105 (p. 14).

[7] Philip Larkin, *Required writing* (London: Faber and Faber, 1983), p. 47.

[8] Gaston Bachlard, *The Poetics Of Space*, trans. by Maria Jolas, 3rd edn. (Boston: Beacon Press, 1994), p. 4.

[9] Bachlard, pp. 4-5.

[10] Andrew Motion, *Philip Larkin: A writer's Life* (London: Faber and Faber, 2nd edn. 1994), p.37.

[11] Soren Kierkegaard, qtd in John Osborne, *Larkin, Ideology, and Critical Violence* (London: Macmillan, 2008), p.93.

[12] Kierkegaard, qtd in Osborne, p. 93.

[13] Tom Paulin, qtd in *Philip Larkin*, ed. by Stephen Regan (London: Macmillan, 1997), p. 164.

[14] Paulin, qtd in Regan, *Philip Larkin*, p.164.

[15] Larkin, qtd in Motion, *Philip Larkin: A Writer's Life*, p.182.

[16] Larkin, qtd in Motion, *A Writer's Life*. P.36.

[17] Lolette Kuby, *An Uncommon Poet For The Common Man* (The Hague-Paris: Mouton, 1974) p. 145.

[18] Osborne, p.105.

[19] Booth, p. 160.

[20] Colin Wilson, *The Outsider* (London: Phoenix, 10th edn., 2001), p. 47.

[21] Philip Larkin, *Further Requirements*, ed. by Anthony Thwaite (London: Faber and Faber, 2002), p. 4.

[22] Wilson, p. 26.

[23] Kierkegaard, qtd in Osborne, p. 90.

[24]

http://www.newi.ac.uk/rdover/larkin/Mr%20Bleaney%20-%20Notes.htmis (accessed 21 August 2011).

[25] Osborne, p. 157.

[26] T.S. Eliot, *The Complete Poems and Plays of T. S Eliot* (London: Faber and Faber, 3rd edn., 1975), p.19.

[27] Jonathan Raban, *The Society of The Poem* (London: George G.Harrap, 1971), p. 30

[28] Raban, p. 30.

[29] Wilson, p.28

[30] Larkin, qtd in Motion, *A Writer's Life*, p.78.

[31] Terry Whalen, *Philip Larkin and English Poetry*, 2nd edn. (London: Macmillan, 1990), p.9.

[32] R.S. Thomas, *Collected Poems* (London: Phoenix, 1993), p. 308.

[33] Thomas, p.46.

[34] Thomas, p. 162.

[35] Thomas,

[36] Andrew Swarbrick, *Out of Reach: The Poetry of Philip Larkin* (London: Macmillan, 1995), p.60.

[37] Charles Tomlinson, qtd in Nicholas Marsh, *Philip Larkin*, (London: Longman,2007), p. 199.

[38] Paulin, qtd in Marsh, *Philip Larkin*, p. 204.

[39] Richard Freeborn, *Turgenev: The Novelist's Novelist* (Oxford: Oxford University Press, 1960), p. 100.

[40] Gianni Vattimo, *The End of Modernity*, trans. by Jon R.Snyder (London: Blackwell, 1991), p. 118.

[41] Whalen, p, 9.

[42] Larkin, qtd in Motion, *Philip Larkin: A Writer's Life*, p.78. [43] Marsh, p.54.

[44] Kuby, p.199.

[45] Larkin, qtd in Kuby, p. 12.

Chapter 2: Transcending sex

[1] Nicholas Marsh, *Philip Larkin* (London: Palgrave 2007), p. 130.

[2]

http://www.time.com/time/magazine/article/0,9171,823 434,00.html#ixzz1WnjytXCW

[3] Andrew Motion, *Philip Larkin* (London: Methuen, 1982), p. 75.

[4] Kuby, p.11.

[5] Kuby p. 1.

[6] Motion, *Philip Larkin*, p. 19.

[7] Simon Petch, *The Art of Philip Larkin* (Sydney: Sydney University Press, 1998), p. 97.

[8] Motion, *Philip Larkin*, p.20.

[9] Larkin, qtd in Rossen, *Philip Larkin*, p. 24

[10] Larkin, qtd in Regan, *Philip Larkin*, p. 140.

[11] Wilson, p. 83.

[12] T. E. Laurence, qtd in Wilson, p.83.

[13] Wilson, p. 83.

[14] Eliot, *The complete poems and plays of T. S Eliot*, p.19.

[15] Philip Larkin, *The Oxford Book of Twentieth-Century English Verse* (Oxford: Oxford University Press, 1973), pp. 228-257.

[16] Larkin, in *Further requirement*, p. 19.

[17] Raphael Ingebien, 'The Use of Symbolism: Larkin and Eliot' qtd in *New Larkins for Old*, ed. by James Booth (London: Palgrave, 2000), pp.130-139, (p.132).

[18] Motion, *A Writer's life*, p. 13.

[19] A.T. Tolley, *My Proper Ground: A Study of the work of Philip Larkin and its development* (Edinburgh: Edinburgh University Press, 1997), p.119.

[20] Marsh, p. 87.

[21] Motion, *A Writer's Life*, p.43.

[22] Philip Shaw, *The Sublime, The New Critical Idiom* (London - New York: Routledge, 2006), p. 30.

[23] M.W. Rowe, Philip Larkin: *Art and Self* (London: Palgrave Macmillan, 2011), pp. 113-114.

[24] Rowe, pp. 113-114.

[25] Rowe, p.114.

Chapter 3: Transcending the ordinary

[1] Kuby, p. 135.

[2] Larkin, *Required Writing*, p. 293.

[3] Larkin, *Required Writing*, p. 252.

[4] Larkin, *Required Writing*, p. 252.

[5] Larkin, *Required Writing*, p.252.

[6] Larkin, qtd in Whalen, *Philip Larkin and English Poetry*, p.96.

[5] Graham Holderness, qtd in Marsh, p. 106.

[6] Terry Whalen, qtd in *New Larkins for Old*, ed. by James Booth (London: Palgrave, 2000), pp. 117- 120 (p.55).

[7] Germaine Greer, qtd in Marsh, p. 200.

[8] James Wood, qtd in Regan, *Philip Larkin*, p. 5.

[9] Andrew Duncan, qtd in Marsh, p. 200.

[10] Martin Amis, 'The Larkin Puzzle', Life & Arts, Financial Times, 20 August, 2011, p.1.

[8] Amis, Financial Times. p.1.

[9] Motion, *Philip Larkin* , p. 78.

[10] Motion, *A Writer's Life,* p. 73.

[11] Larkin, qtd in (Graham Chesters, Tireless play: speculations on Larkin's 'Absences') http://www.philiplarkin.com/pdfs/essays/absences_gchesters.pdf (accessed 3 Augest2011)

[17] Larkin, qtd in Booth, p.162.

[18] Swarbrick, p. 68.

[19] Immanuel Kant, qtd in Rowe, p.133.

[20] Marjorie Perloff, *Frank O'Hara*: *Poet Among Painters* 2nd edn. (Chicago: University of Chicago, 1977), p.21.

[21] Perloff, *Frank O'Hara: Poet Among Painters*, p.21.

[22] Maurice Merleau–Ponty, *The Primacy of Perception*, ed. by James M.Edie 2nd edn. (New York: Northwestern Press, 1968), p.6.

[23] Ponty, p.6.

[24] Frank O'Hara, *Selected Poems* (New York: Alfred A. Knope, 2009), p. 6.

[25] Larkin, qtd in Andrew Gibson, 'Larkin and Ordinaries', in *Philip Larkin: The Poems* (London: Longman) pp. 9-18 (p. 13).

[26] Rowe, p.26.

[27] Tolley, p. 104.

[28] Roger Day, *Larkin* (London: Open University Press, 1987), p. 54.

[29] Booth, p.164.

[30] Rowe, p. 15.

[31] Rowe, p.9.

[32] Petch, p.80.

[36] Osborne, p.147.

[33] Osborne, p. 148.

[34] Fredric Jameson, qtd in Mark Silverberg, *The New York School Poets and the Neo-Avant–Garde* (Ottawa: Cape Breton University, 2010), p.103.

[35] Eliot, *The Complete Poems and Plays*, p.19.

[36] Swarbrick, p.103.

[37] Rowe, p.23.

[38] Rowe, p.23.

[39] Rowe, p.25.

[40] Tolley, p. 105.

[41] Swarbrick, p.150.

[42] Rossen, p.55.

[43] Seamus Heaney, 'The Main of Light' in *Philip Larkin*, ed. by Stephen Rogan (London: Macmillan, 1997), pp. 23-31(p.26).

Bibliography

Amis, Martin, 'The Larkin Puzzle', Life & Arts, Financial Times, 20 August, 2011.

Bachlard, Gaston, *The Poetics Of Space*, trans. by Maria Jolas, 3rd edn. (Boston: Beacon Press, 1994).

Booth, James, *Philip Larkin* (New York, London: Harvester Wheatsheaf, 1992).

Day, Roger, *Larkin* (London: Open University Press, 1987).

Dunayveskaya Raya in http://www.marxists.org/archive/dunayevskaya/works/phil-rev/dunayev6.htm   (accessed 21 August 201).

Eliot T.S. *The Complete Poems and Plays of T. S Eliot* (London: Faber and Faber, 3rd edn., 1975).

Freeborn Richard, *Turgenev: The Novelist's Novelist* (Oxford: Oxford University Press, 1960).

Gibson, Andrew 'Larkin and Ordinaries', in *Philip Larkin: The Poems* (London: Longman) pp. 9-18.

Hedgecock, Liz, in *New Larkins For Old*, pp. 97-105.

81

Heaney, Seamus, 'The Main of Light' in *Philip Larkin*, ed. by Stephen Rogan (London: Macmillan, 1997), pp. 23-31.

Ingebien, Raphael, 'The Use of Symbolism: Larkin and Eliot' qtd in *New Larkins for Old*, ed. by James Booth (London: Palgrave, 2000), pp.130-139, (p.132).

Larkin, Philip, *Collected Poems*, ed. by Anthony Thwaite (London: Faber and Faber, 1988).

Larkin, Philip, *Required Writing* (London: Faber and Faber, 1983).

Kent, Immanuel Kant, qtd. in *Art and Self.*

Kuby, Lolette, *An Uncommon Poet For The Common Man* (The Hague-Paris: Mouton, 1974)

Marsh, Nicholas, *Philip Larkin: The Poems* (London: Palgrave & Macmillan, 2007).

Merleau–Ponty, Maurice *The Primacy of Perception*, ed.by James M.Edie 2nd edn. (New York: Northwestern Press, 1968).

Motion, Andrew, *Philip Larkin*: *A writer's Life* (London: Faber and Faber, 2nd edn. 1994).

O'Hara Frank, *Selected Poems* (New York: Alfred A. Knope, 2009).

Paulin, Tom, qtd in Regan, p.23.

Perloff, Marjorie, *Frank O'Hara: Poet Among Painters* 2nd edn. (Chicago: University of Chicago, 1977).

Petch, Simon, *The Art of Philip Larkin* (Sydney: Sydney University Press, 1998).

Raban, Jonathan, *The Society of The Poem* (London: George G.Harrap, 1971).

Rossen, Janice 'Difficulties with Girls' in *Philip Larkin*, ed. Stephen Regan (London: Macmillan, 1997), pp: 135-159.

Thomas, R.S. *Collected Poems* (London: Phoenix, 1993), (Macmillan, 1997, 138).

Tomlinson, Charles, qtd. in Nicholas Marsh, *Philip Larkin* (London: Palgrave 2007).

Tolley, A.T., *My Proper Ground: A Study of the work of Philip Larkin and its development* (Edinburgh: Edinburgh University Press, 1997).

Vattimo, Gianni, *The End of Modernity*, trans. by Jon R.Snyder (London: Blackwell, 1991).

Whalen, Terry, in *New Larkins for Old*, ed. by James Booth (London: Palgrave, 2000), pp. 117- 120 (p.113).

Wilson, Colin, *The Outsider* (London: Phoenix, 10th edn. 2001).